AF632059

Magnus Wennman

# WHERE THE CHILDREN SLEEP

KEHRER

One misses his own bed. Another, her doll with the dark eyes. A third dreams himself back to a time when his pillow was not an enemy.

The war in Syria has continued for five years, and more than two million children are fleeing the conflict, within and outside the country's borders. They have left their friends, their homes, and their beds behind. A few of these children offered to show us where they sleep now, when everything that once was no longer exists.

# Lamar

### 5 years old

**HORGOŠ, SERBIA.** Back home in Baghdad, the dolls, the toy train, and the ball have been left behind; Lamar often talks about these items when home is mentioned. The bomb changed everything. The family was on its way to buy food when it dropped close to their house. “It was not possible to live there anymore,” says Sara, Lamar’s grandmother. After two attempts to cross the sea from Turkey in a small rubber boat, they succeeded in coming here to Hungary’s closed border. Now Lamar sleeps on a blanket in the forest scared, frozen, and sad.

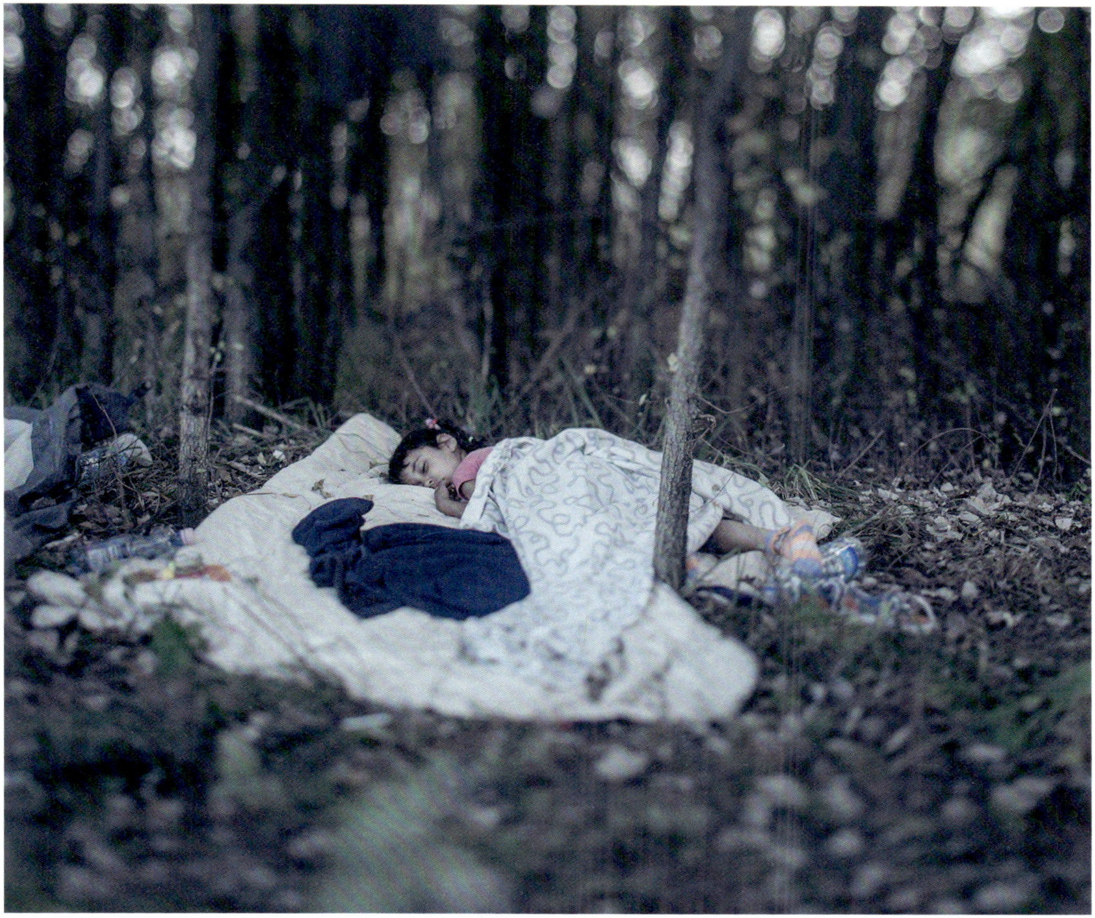

# Mahdi

18 months old

**HORGOŠ / RÖSZKE, SERBIAN-HUNGARIAN BORDER.** Mahdi has experienced only war and flight. He sleeps deeply, despite the hundreds of refugees climbing around him. They are protesting against not being able to travel further through Hungary. On the other side of the border, hundreds of police are standing. They have orders from Prime Minister Viktor Orbán to protect the border at all costs. The situation is becoming more desperate, and the day after the photo is taken, the police use tear gas and water cannons against the refugees.

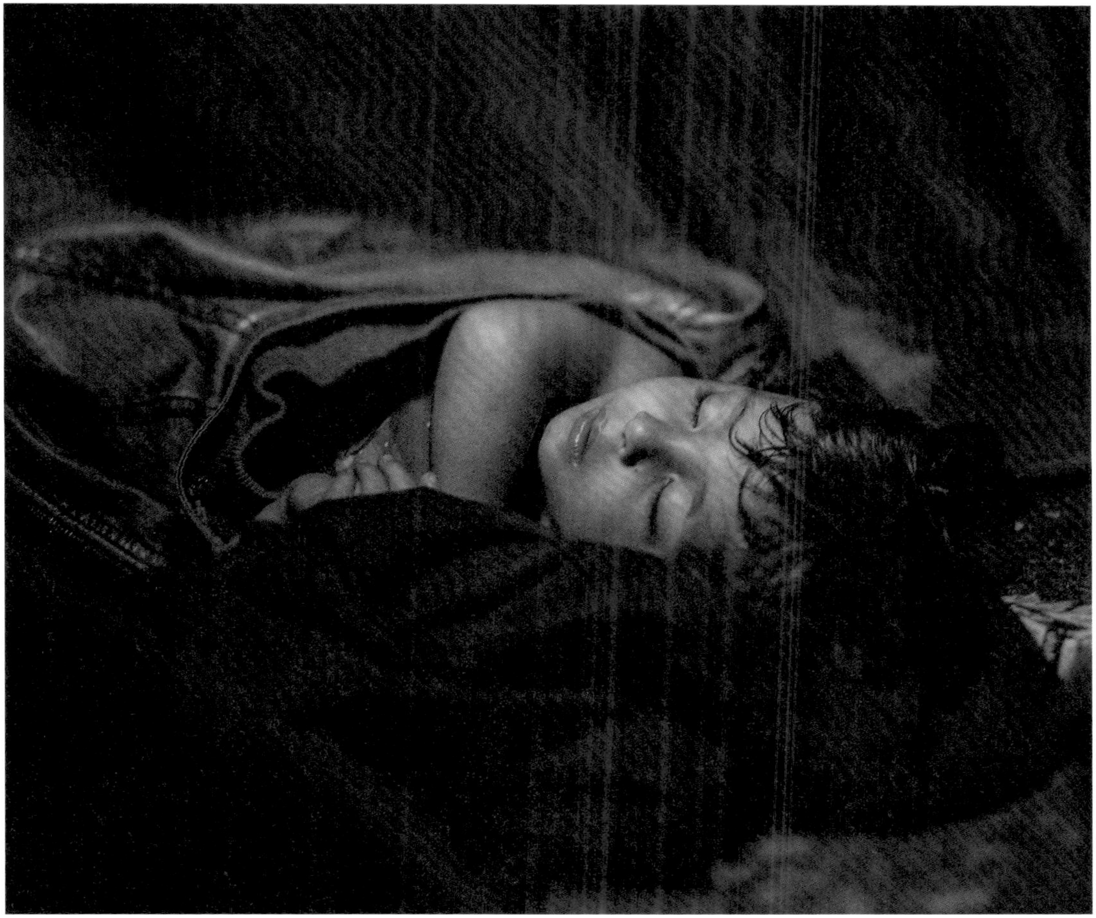

# Abdul Karim

17 years old

**ATHENS, GREECE.** Abdul Karim Addo has no money left. He bought a ferry ticket to Athens with his last euros. Now he spends the night on Omonoia Square, where hundreds of refugees arrive each day. Here, smugglers make big money organizing false passports, as well as bus and plane tickets for refugees—but Abdul Karim is not going anywhere. He is able to borrow a telephone and calls home to his mother in Syria, but he is not able to tell her how bad things are. “She cries and is scared for my sake, and I don’t want to worry her more.” He unfolds his blanket in the middle of the square and curls up in the fetal position. “I dream of two things: to sleep in a bed again and to hug my younger sister.”

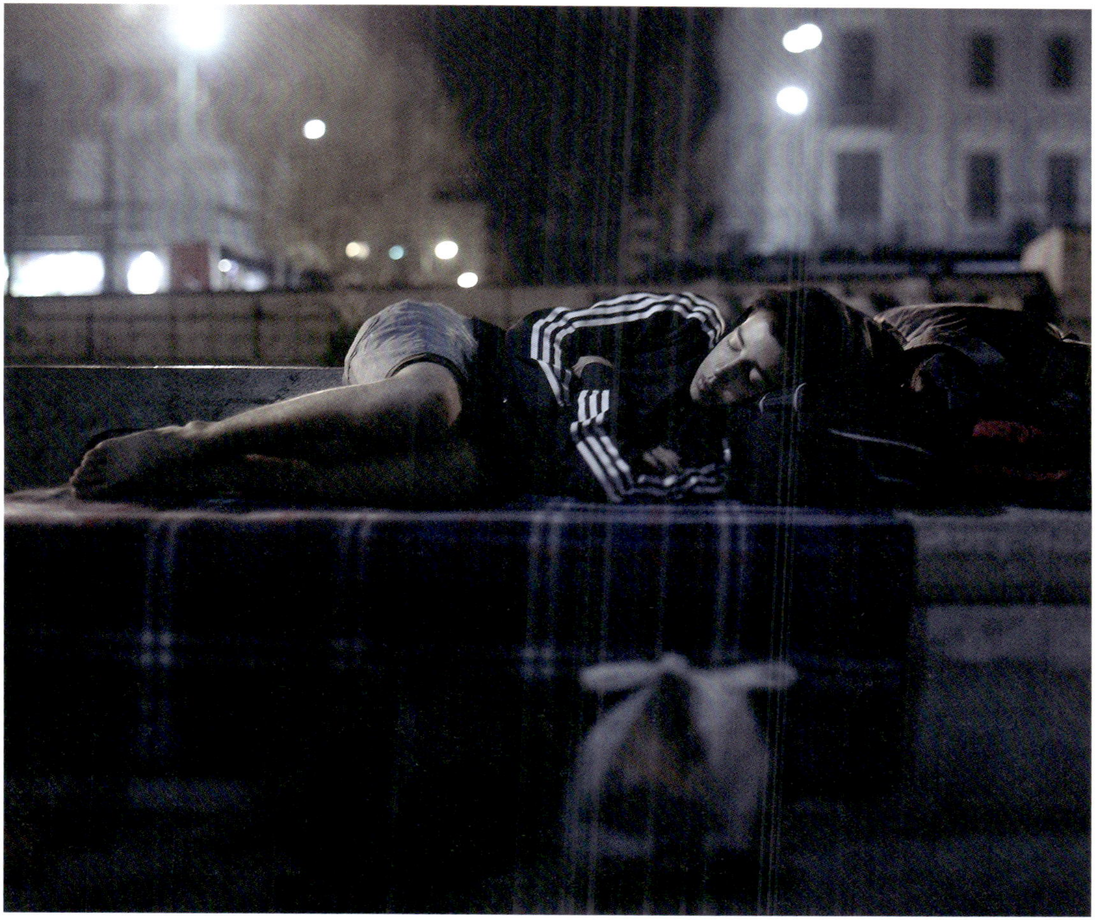

## Ahmad

7 years old

**HORGOŠ / RÖSZKE, SERBIAN-HUNGARIAN BORDER.** Even sleep is not a free zone; it is then that the terror replays. Ahmad was home when the bomb hit his family's house in Idlib. Shrapnel hit him in the head, but he survived. His younger brother did not. The family had lived with war as their nearest neighbor for several years. But without a home, they had no choice. They were forced to flee. Now Ahmad lies among thousands of other refugees on the asphalt along the highway leading to Hungary's closed border. This is day sixteen of their flight. The family has slept in bus shelters, on the road, and in the forest, Ahmad's father explains.

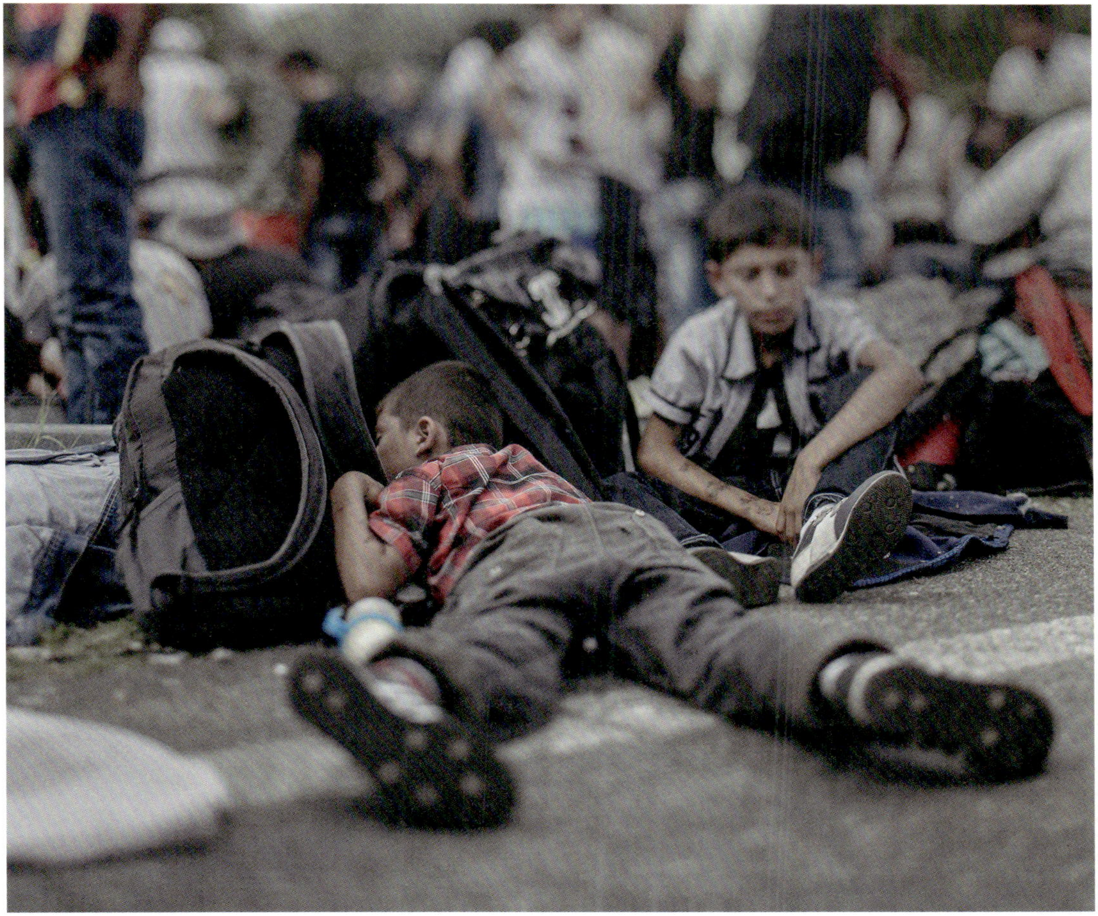

# Shehd

7 years old

**HORGOŠ / RÖSZKE, SERBIAN-HUNGARIAN BORDER.** Shehd loves to draw; but more recently, all of her drawings have had the same theme: weapons. “She saw them all the time; they are everywhere,” explains her mother while the little girl sleeps on the ground alongside Hungary’s closed border. Now she does not draw at all. The family brought neither paper nor crayons with them on their flight. Shehd does not play anymore either. The escape has forced children to become adults and share concern for what happens in an hour or a day. The family has had difficulty finding food during their long trek. Some days, they have had to make do with apples they were able to pick from trees along the road. If the family had known how hard the journey would be, they would have chosen to risk their lives in Syria.

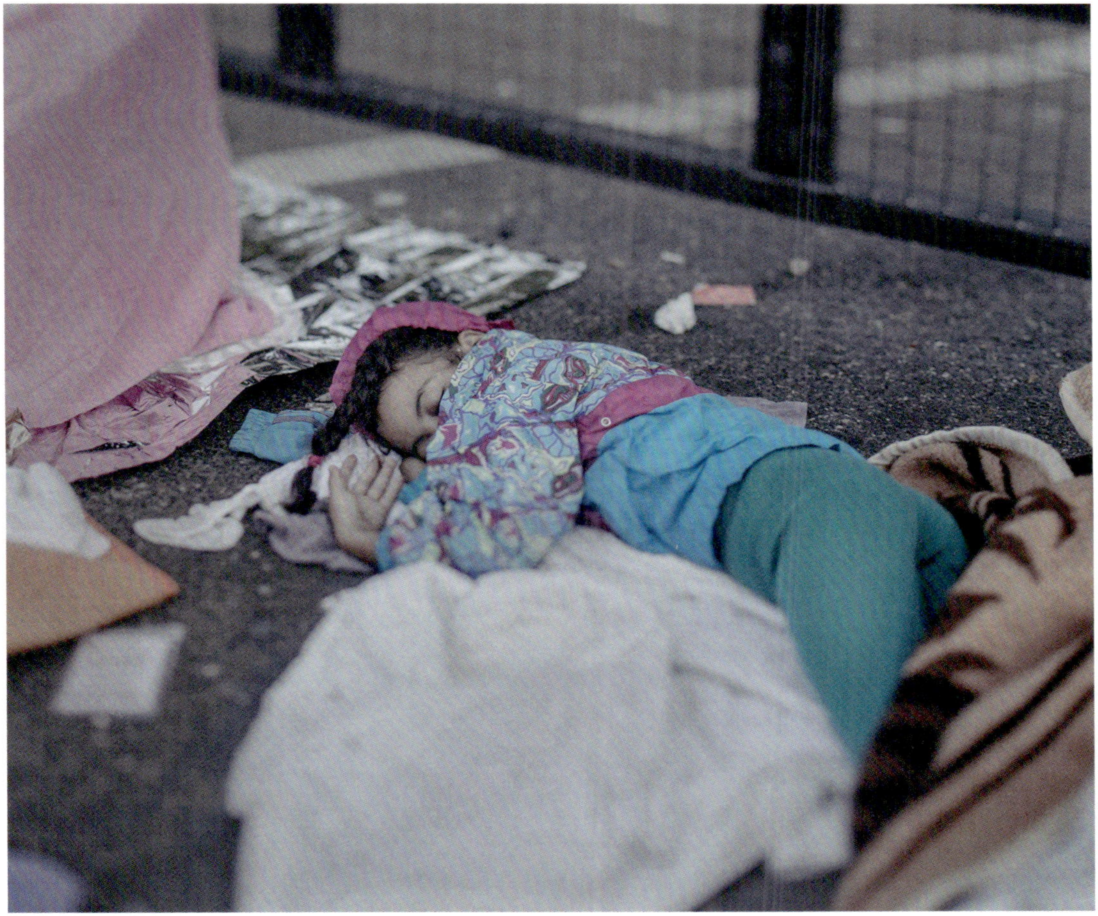

## Sham

1 year old

**HORGOŠ / RÖSZKE, SERBIAN-HUNGARIAN BORDER.** In the very front, just alongside the border between Serbia and Hungary near the four-meter-high iron gate, Sham is lying in his mother's arms. Just a few decimeters behind them is the Europe they are so desperately trying to reach. Only one day before, the last refugees were allowed through and taken by train to Austria. But Sham and his mother arrived too late, along with thousands of other refugees, who now wait outside the closed Hungarian border.

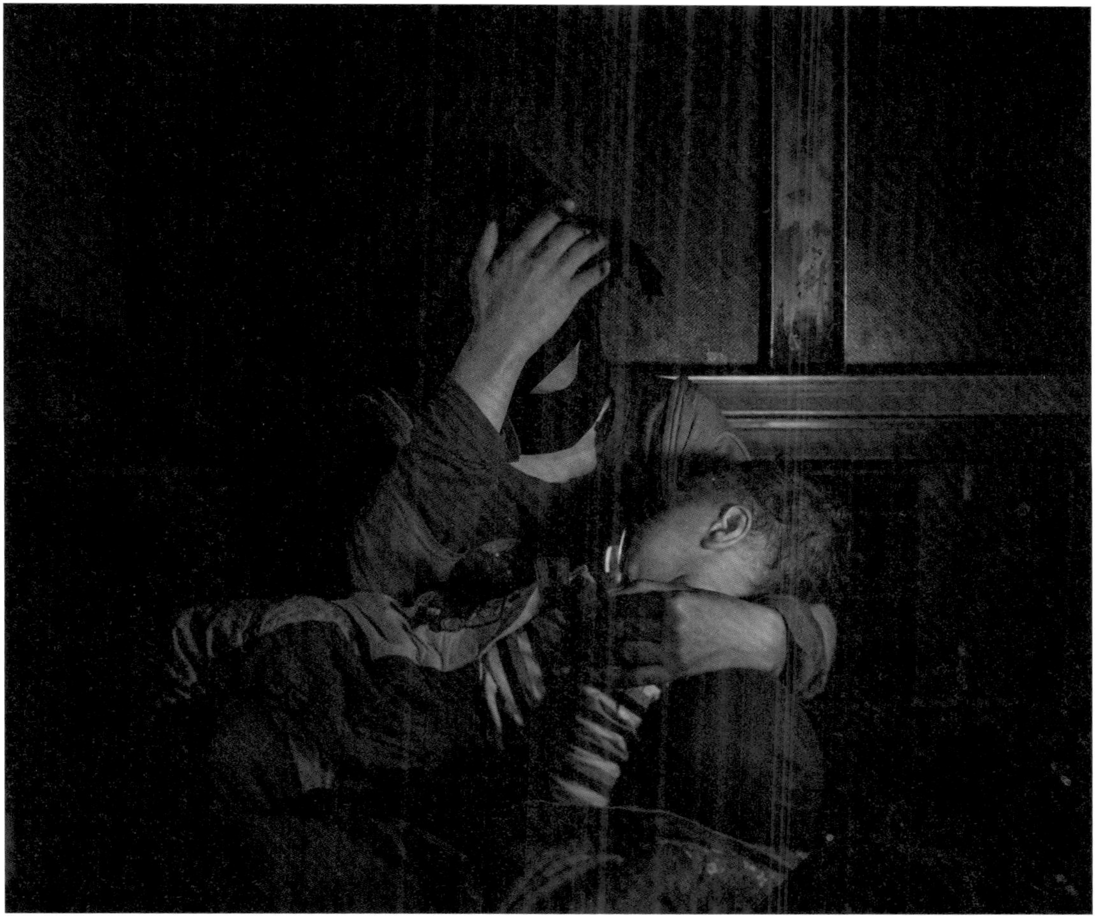

# Abdullah

5 years old

**BELGRADE, SERBIA**. Abdullah has a blood disease. For the last two days, he has been sleeping outside of the central station in Belgrade. He witnessed the killing of his sister in their home in Daraa. “He is still in shock and has nightmares every night,” says his mother. Abdullah is tired and is not healthy, but his mother does not have the money to buy him medicine.

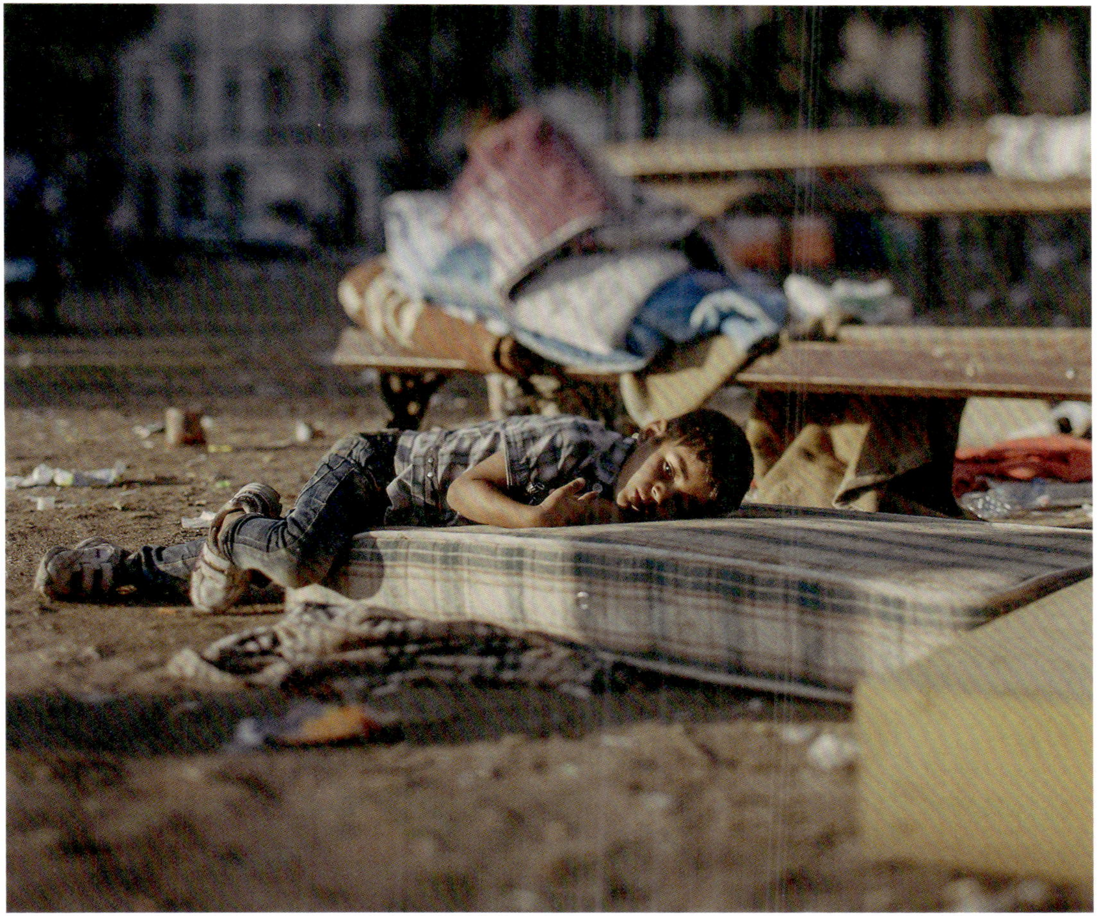

# Juliana

2 years old

**HORGOŠ, SERBIA.** It is 34 degrees Celsius. The flies crawl on Juliana's face, and she shifts uneasily in her sleep. Juliana's family has been walking through Serbia for two days. This is the latest phase of a flight that began three months ago. The girl's mother lays her thin shawl over her daughter lying on the ground. Juliana calms down. A few meters away from their resting place, feet are tramping by in a neverending flow of people. It is the end of August and Hungary is about to barricade itself with barbed wire to shut out this stream of refugees. But for a few more days, it is possible to pass through the border city of Horgoš. As soon as evening comes, Juliana's family will try to move on.

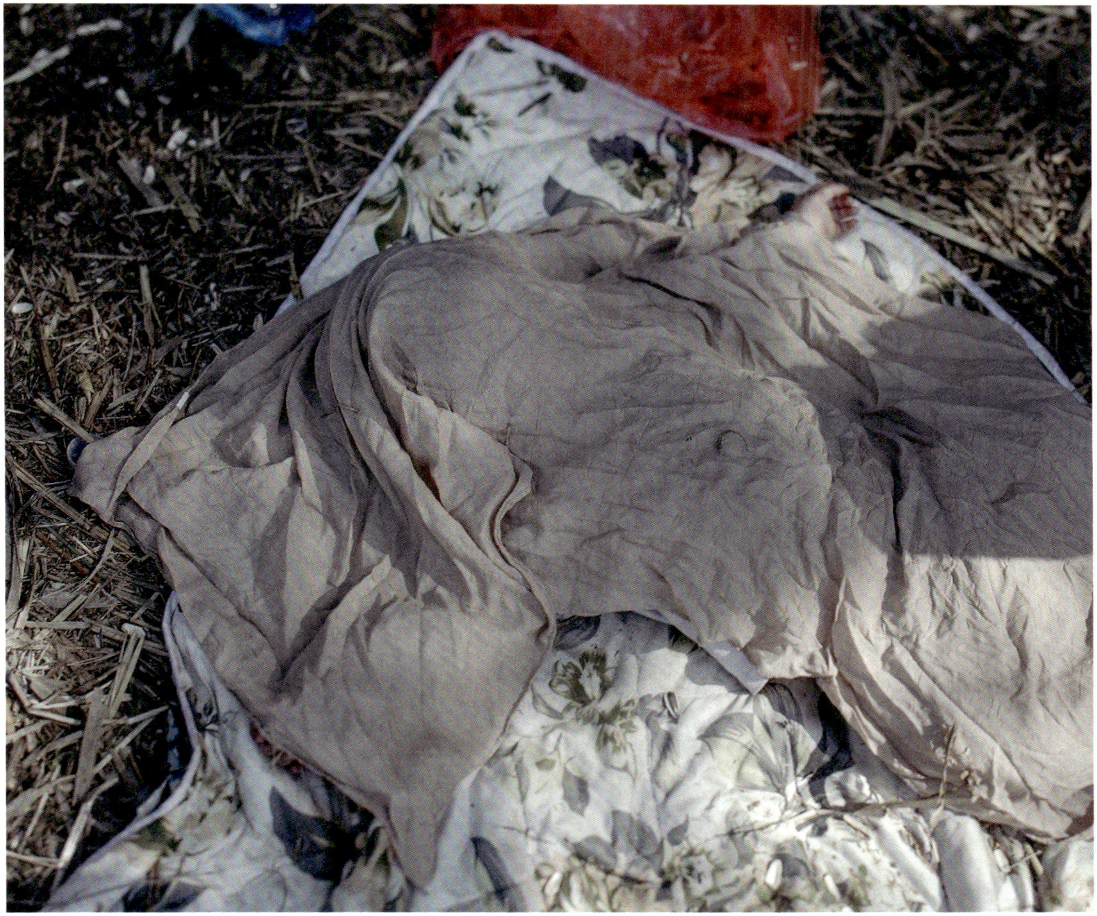

# Ahmed

## 6 years old

**HORGOŠ, SERBIA.** It is after midnight when Ahmed falls asleep in the grass. The adults are still sitting around, formulating plans for how they are going to get into Hungary. Ahmed is six years old and carries his own bag over the long stretches that his family walks by foot. “He is brave and only cries sometimes in the evenings,” says his uncle, who has taken care of Ahmed since his father was killed in their hometown of Deir ez-Zor in northern Syria.

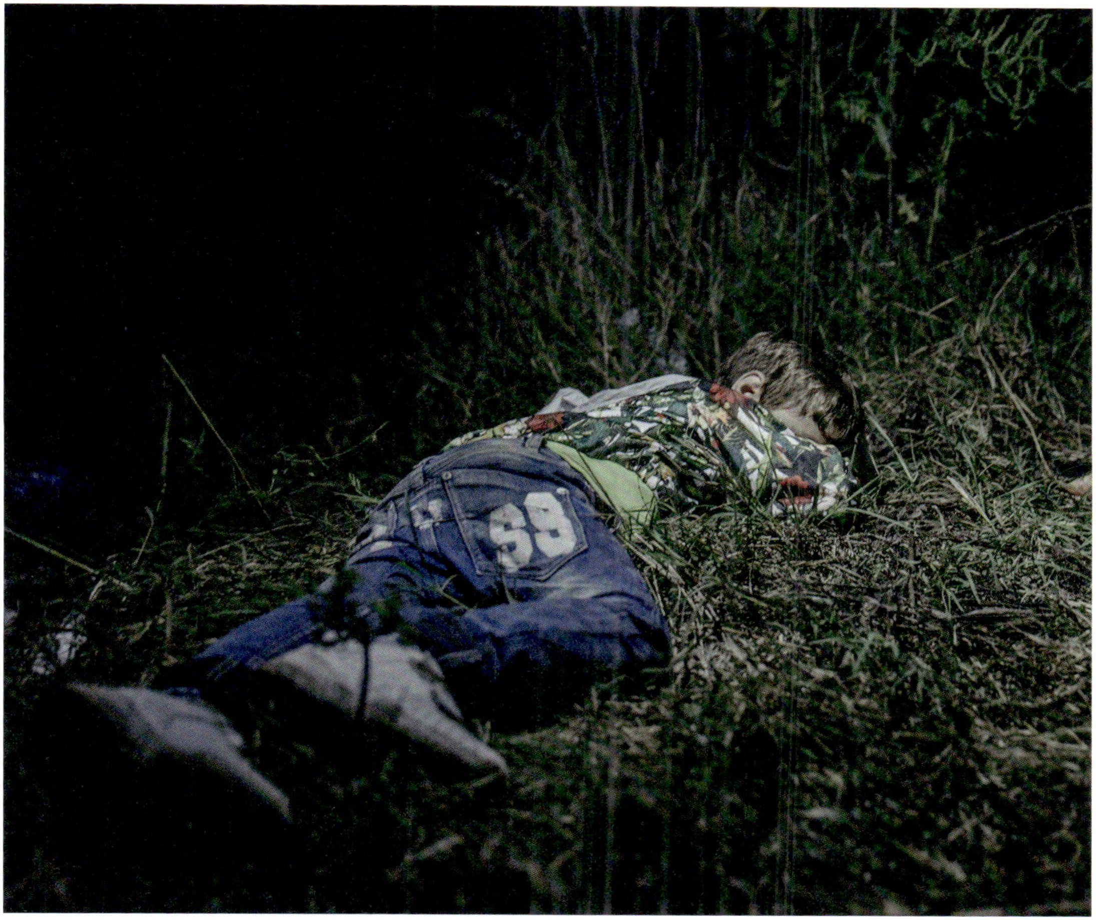

# Shiraz

9 years old

**SURUÇ, TURKEY.** Shiraz was only three months old when she was stricken with a severe fever. The doctor diagnosed polio and advised her parents to not spend too much money on medicine for the girl who “didn’t have a chance.” Then the war came. Her mother, Leila, starts crying when she describes how she wrapped the girl in a blanket and carried her over the border from Kobanî to Turkey. Shiraz, who can’t talk, received a wooden cradle in the refugee camp. She lies there day and night.

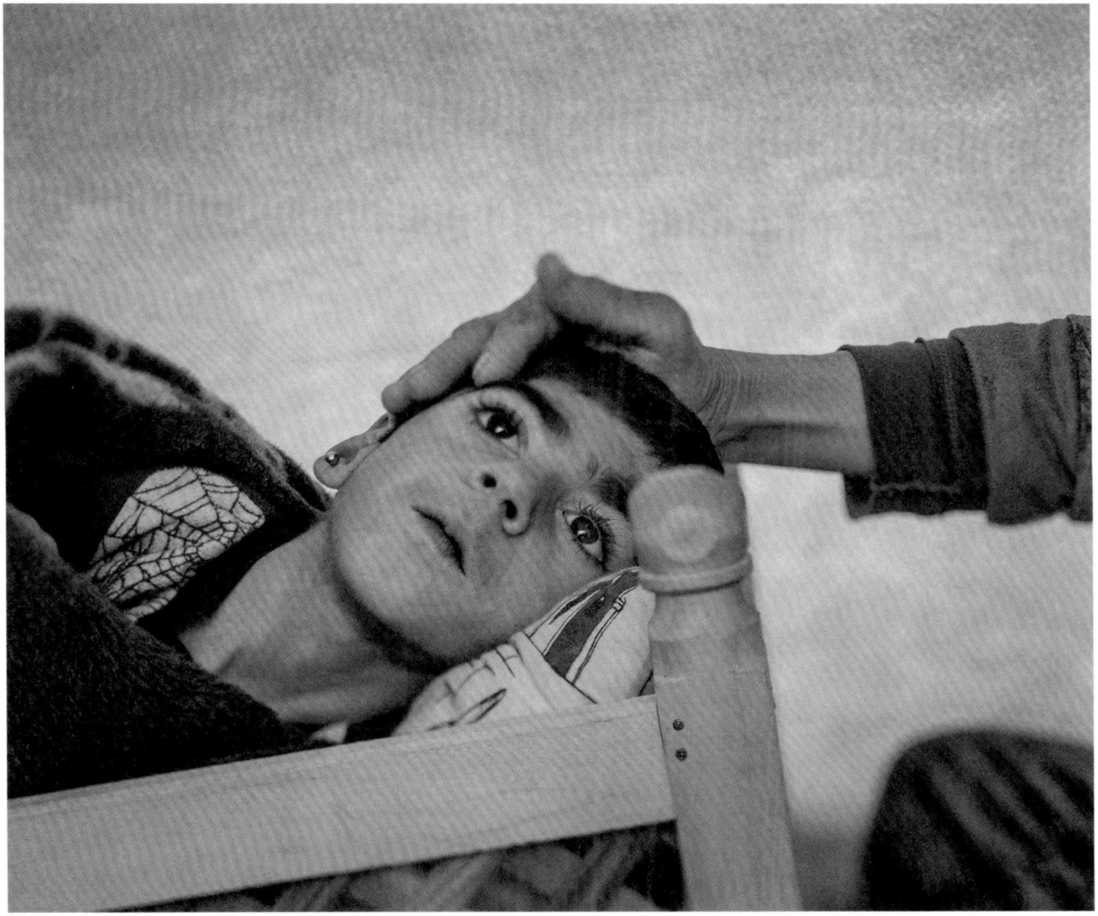

## Mohammed

13 years old

**NIZIP, TURKEY.** Mohammed loves houses. Back home in Aleppo, he used to enjoy walking around the city looking at them. Now, many of his favorite buildings are gone—blown to pieces. Lying in his hospital bed, he wonders whether he will ever fulfill his dream of becoming an architect. “The strangest thing about war is that you get used to feeling scared. I wouldn’t have believed that,” says Mohammed.

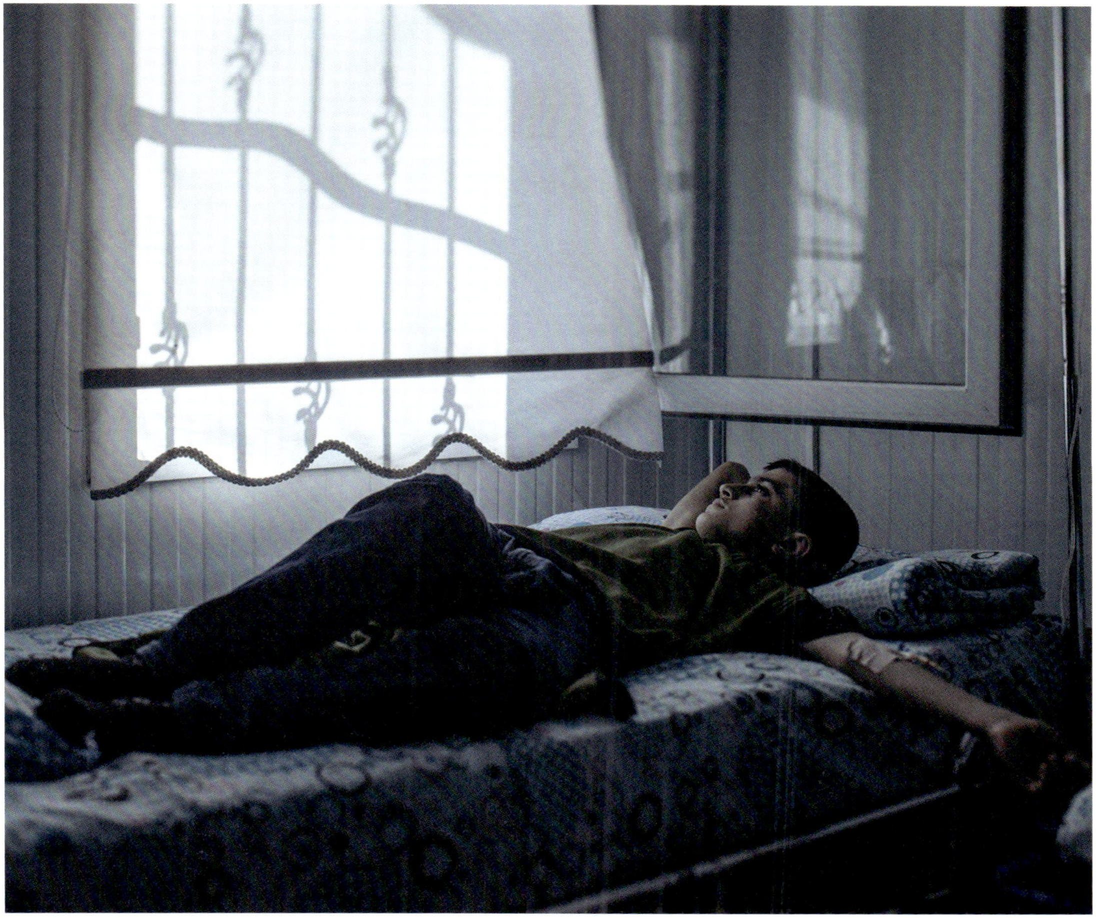

# Iman

2 years old

**AZRAQ, JORDAN.** Iman has pneumonia and a chest infection. This is her third day in this hospital bed. “She sleeps most of the time now. Normally, she’s a happy little girl; but now she’s tired. She runs everywhere when she’s well. She loves playing in the sand,” says her mother, Olah, 19.

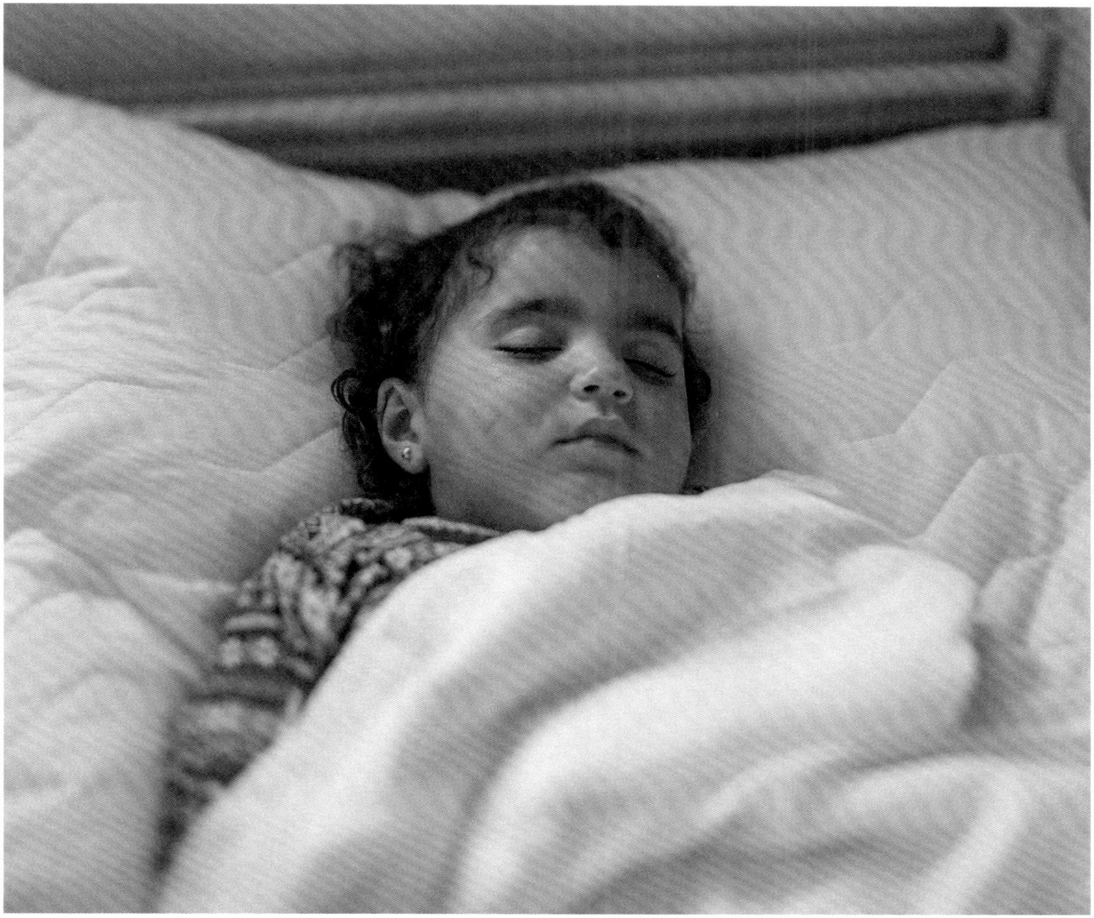

# Gulistan

6 years old

**SURUÇ, TURKEY.** There's a difference between closing your eyes and sleeping, as six-year-old Gulistan knows. She prefers to shut her eyes and just pretend, because every time she really falls asleep, the nightmares start again. "I don't want to sleep here. I want to sleep at home," she says. She misses the pillow she had in Kobanî. Sometimes she lies against her mother and uses her as a pillow.

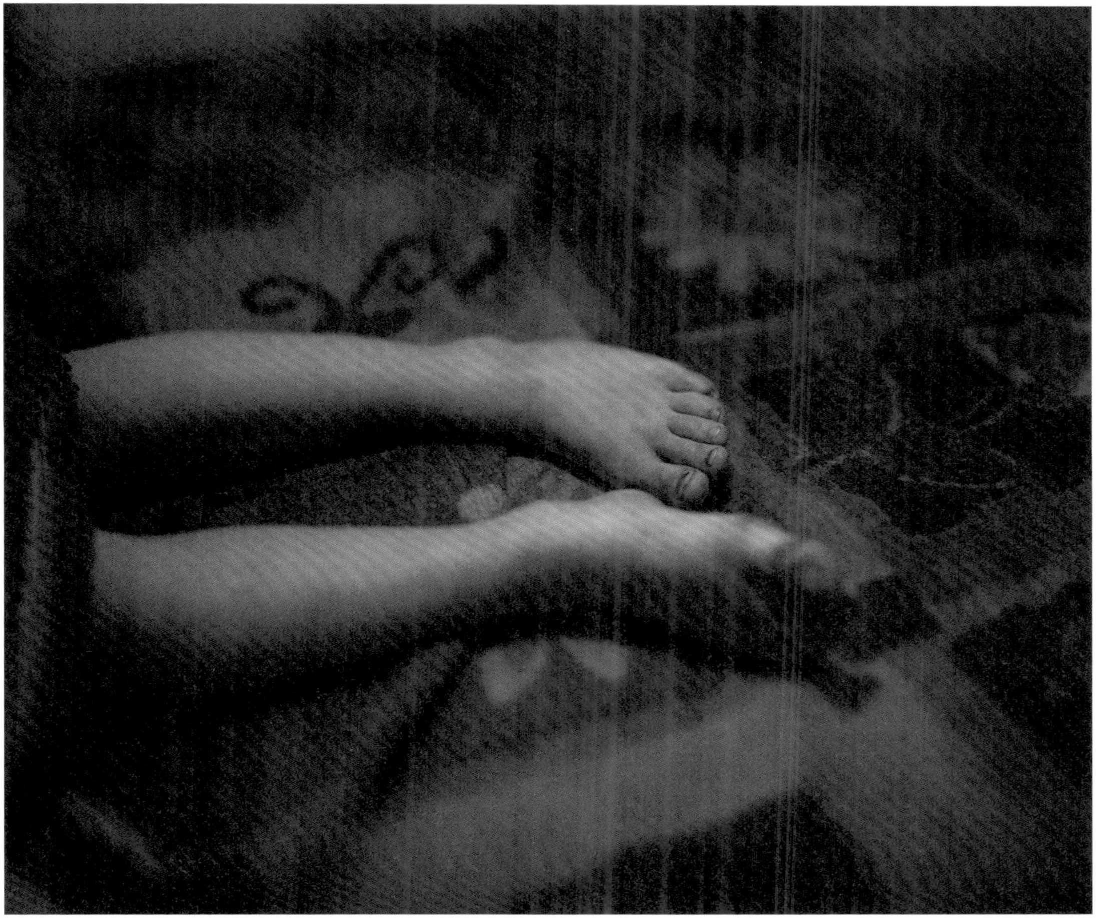

# Tamam

5 years old

**AZRAQ, JORDAN.** Tamam is scared of her pillow. She cries every night at bedtime. The air raids on her hometown of Homs usually took place at night, and although she has been sleeping away from home for nearly two years now, she still doesn’t realize that her pillow is not the source of danger.

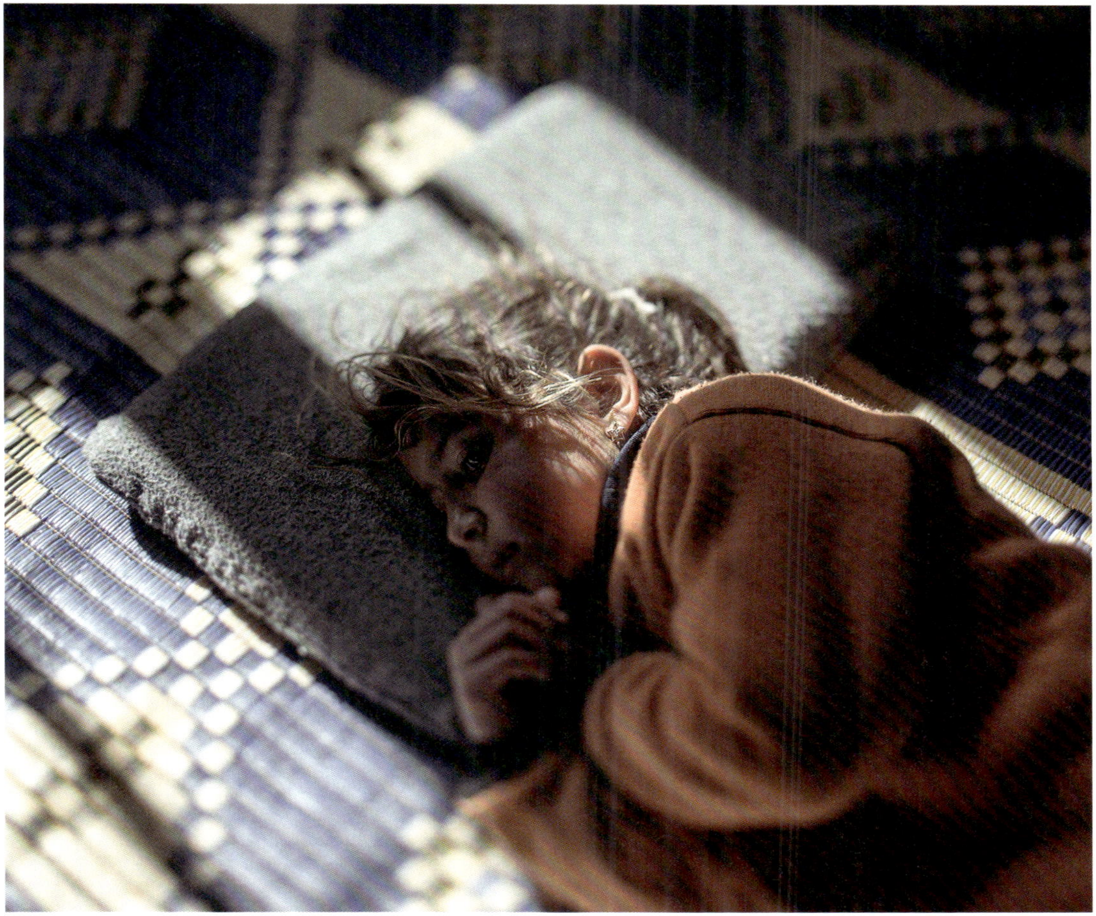

| Esra | Esma | Sidra |
|---|---|---|
| 11 years old | 8 years old | 6 years old |

**AMMAN, JORDAN.** When Selam, 37, puts Esra, Esma, and Sidra to bed, she takes comfort from the knowledge that her children are safe and won't come under attack during the night. What saddens her is the fact that they constantly dream about their father, who disappeared after being abducted, and wake up distraught. "I often dream that Daddy is bringing me candy," says Sidra.

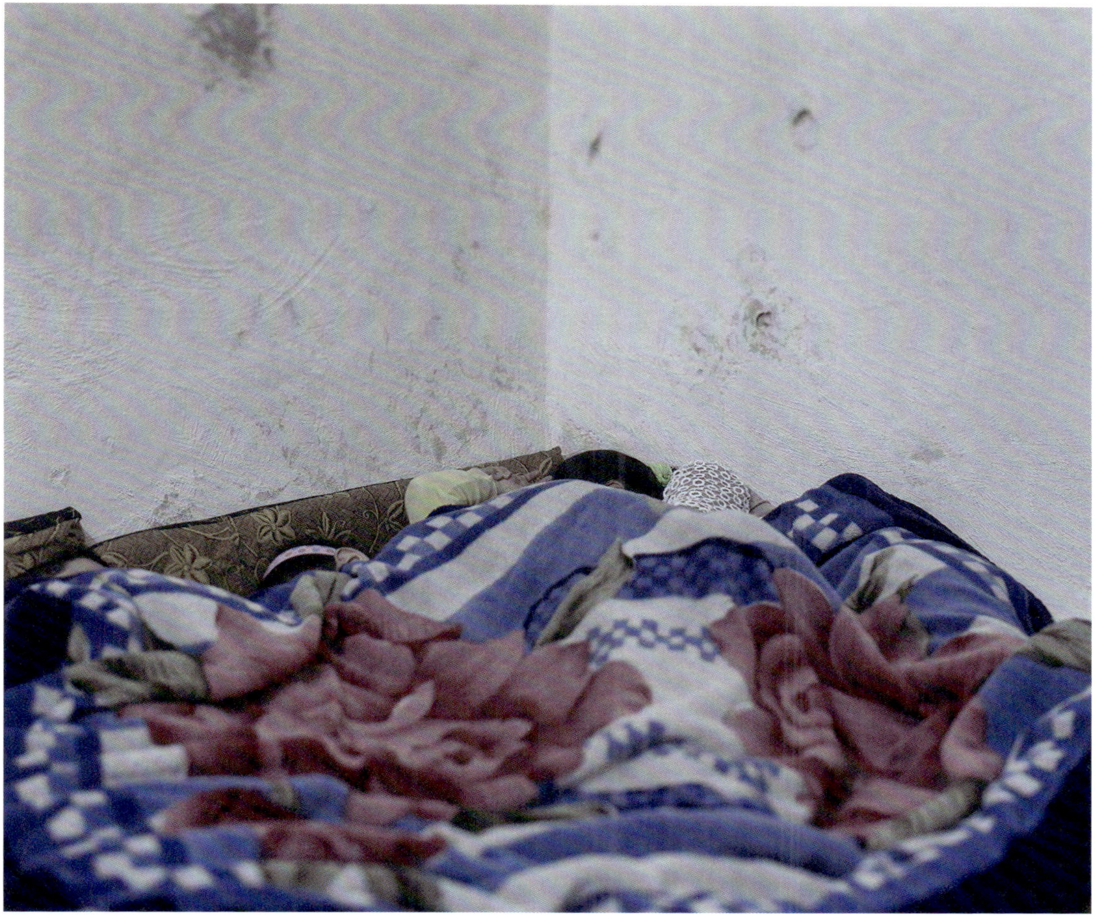

## Maram

8 years old

**AMMAN, JORDAN.** Maram had just come home from school when the rocket hit her house. A piece of the roof landed right on top of her. Her mother took her to a field hospital, and from there she was airlifted across the border to Jordan. Head trauma caused a brain hemorrhage. For the first eleven days, Maram was in a coma. She is now conscious, but has a broken jaw and can’t speak.

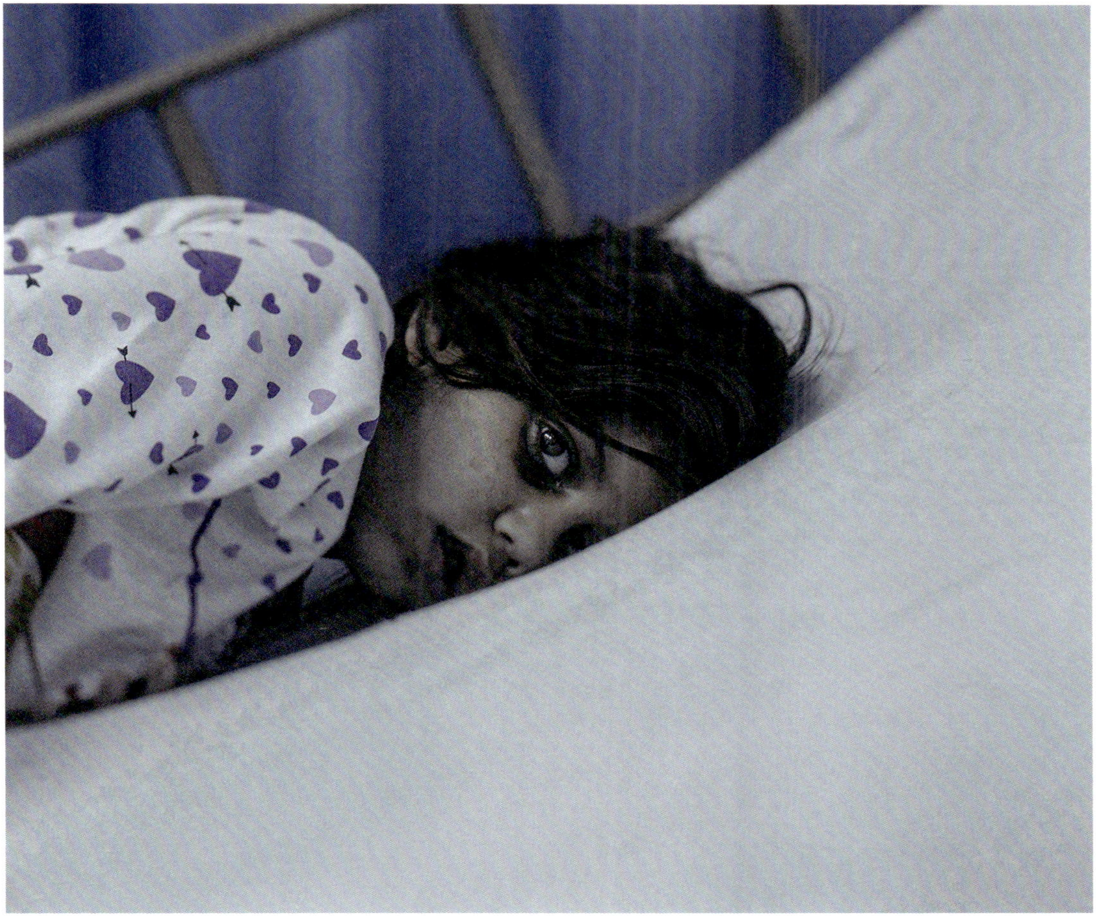

## Ralia
7 years old

## Rahaf
13 years old

**BEIRUT, LEBANON.** Ralia and Rahaf live on the streets of Beirut. They are from Damascus, where a grenade killed their mother and brother. Along with their father, they have been sleeping there roughly for a year. They huddle close together on their cardboard boxes. Rahaf says she is scared of “bad boys,” and Ralia starts crying.

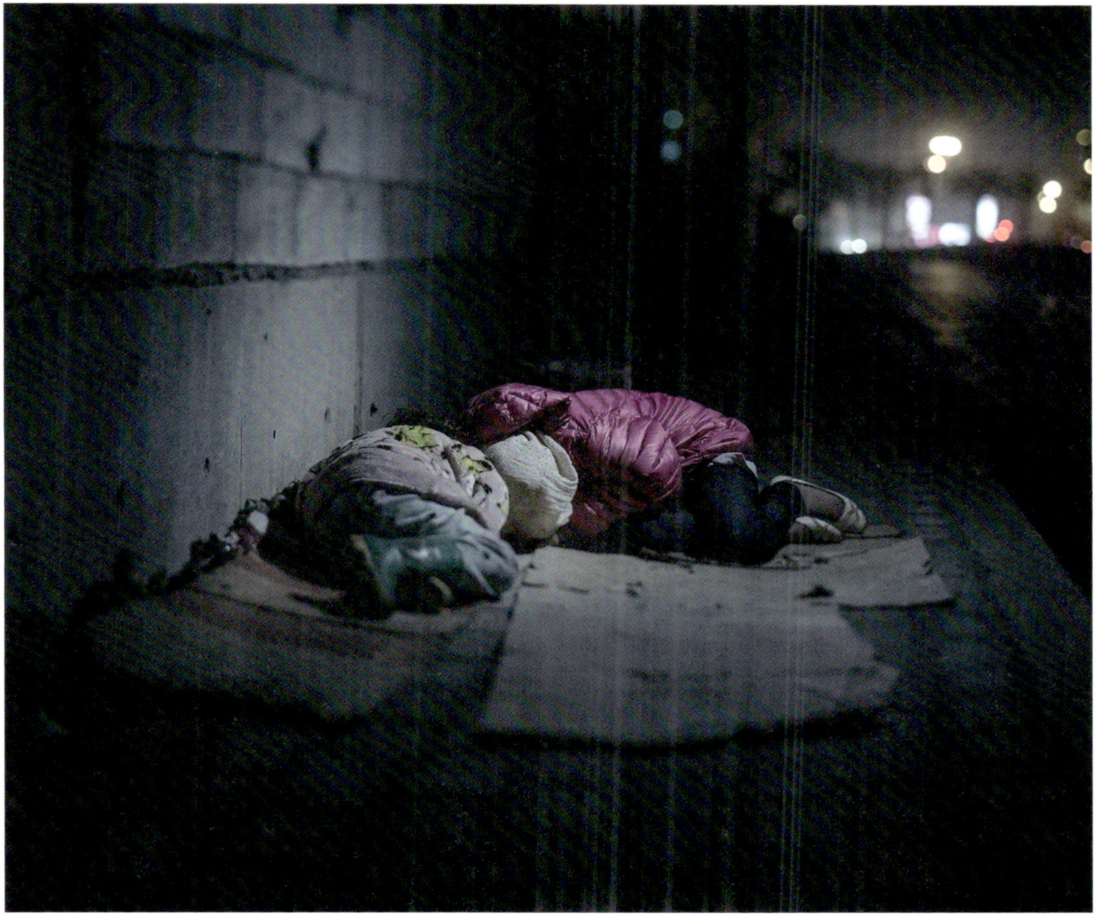

## Moyad

5 years old

**AMMAN, JORDAN.** Moyad and his mother needed to buy flour to make a spinach pie. Hand in hand, they were on their way to the market in Daraa. They walked past a taxi, in which someone had placed a bomb. Moyad's mother died instantly. The boy, who has been airlifted to Jordan, has shrapnel lodged in his head, back, and pelvis.

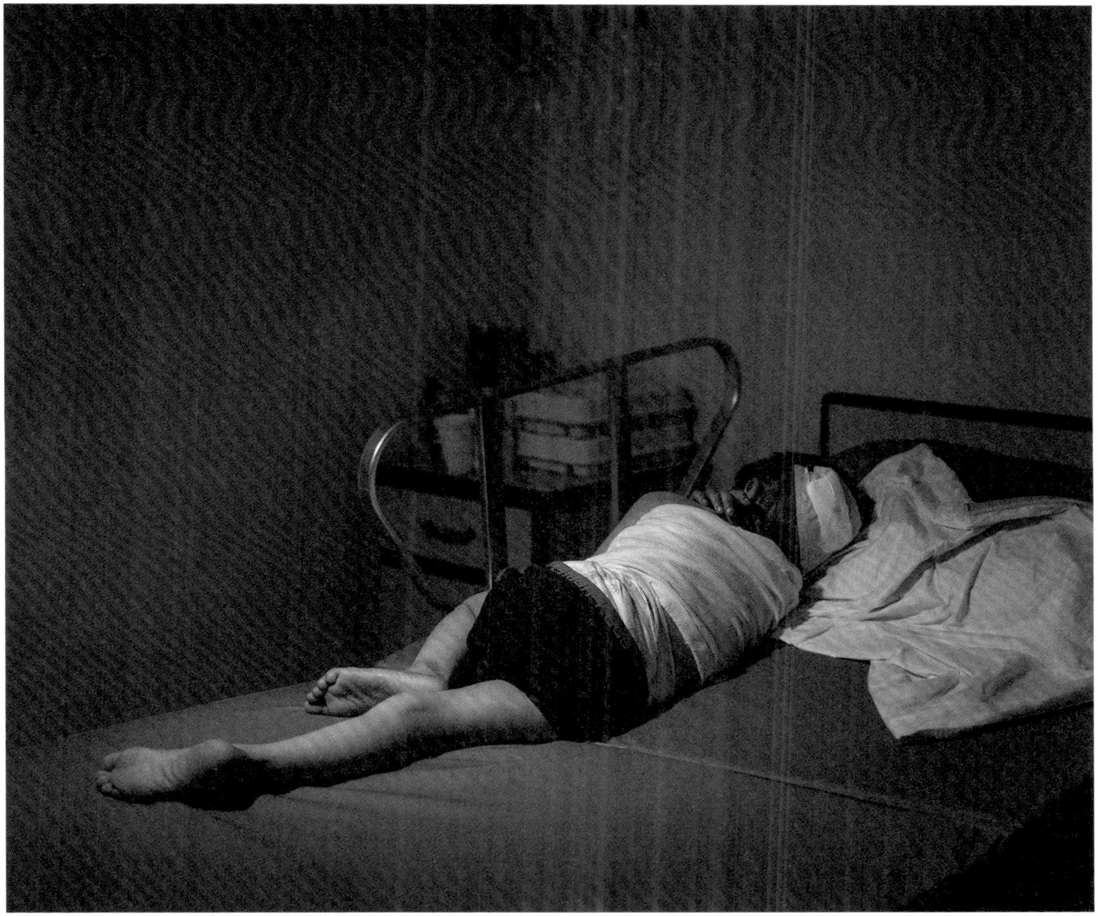

# Walaa

5 years old

**DAR-EL-IAS, LEBANON.** Walaa wants to go home. She had her own room in Aleppo, she tells us. There, she never used to cry at bedtime. Here, in the refugee camp, she cries every night. Resting her head on the pillow is horrible, she says, because nighttime is horrible. That was when the attacks happened. By day, Walaa's mother often builds a little house out of pillows, to teach her that they are nothing to be afraid of.

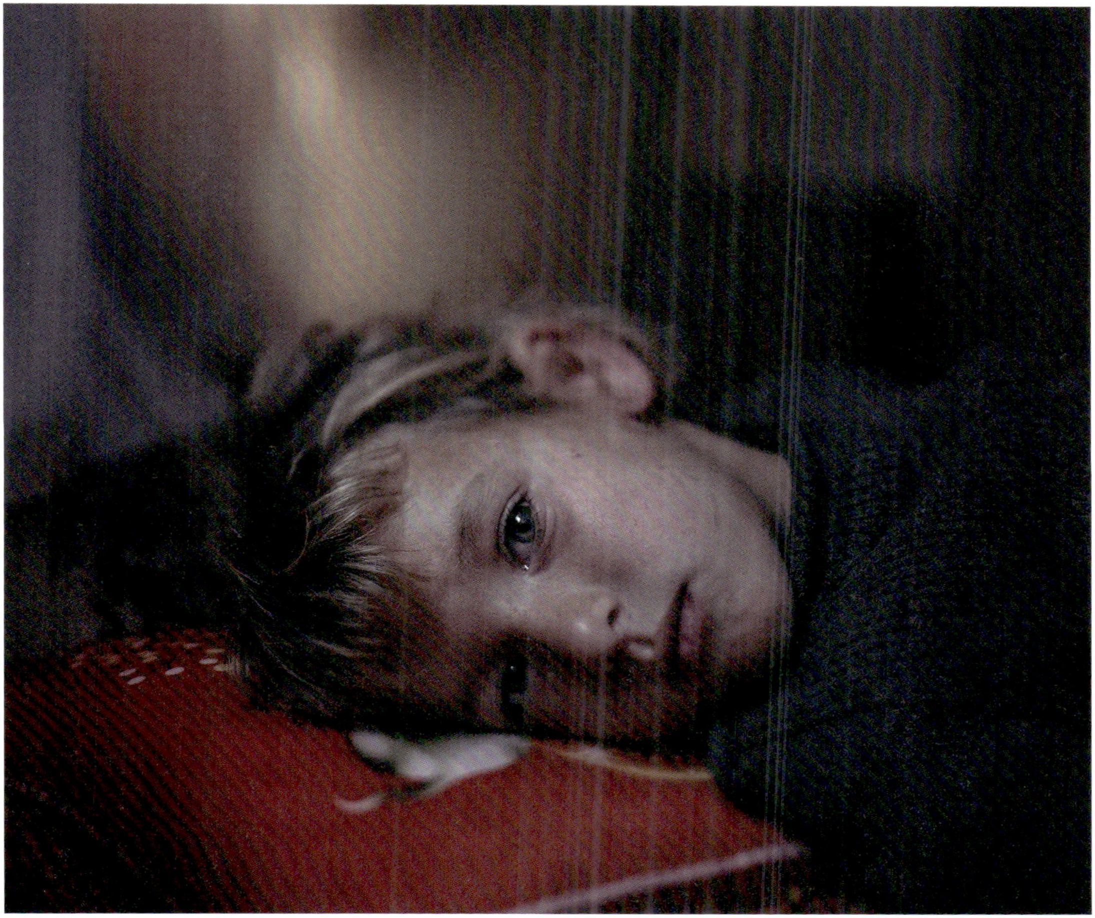

## Amir

20 months old

**FAYDA NEAR ZAHLÉ, LEBANON.** Amir was born a refugee. His mother believes her son was traumatized in the womb. “Amir has never spoken a single word,” says Shahana, 32. In the plastic tent where the family now lives, Amir has no toys, but he plays with whatever he can find on the ground. “He laughs a lot, even though he doesn’t talk,” says his mother.

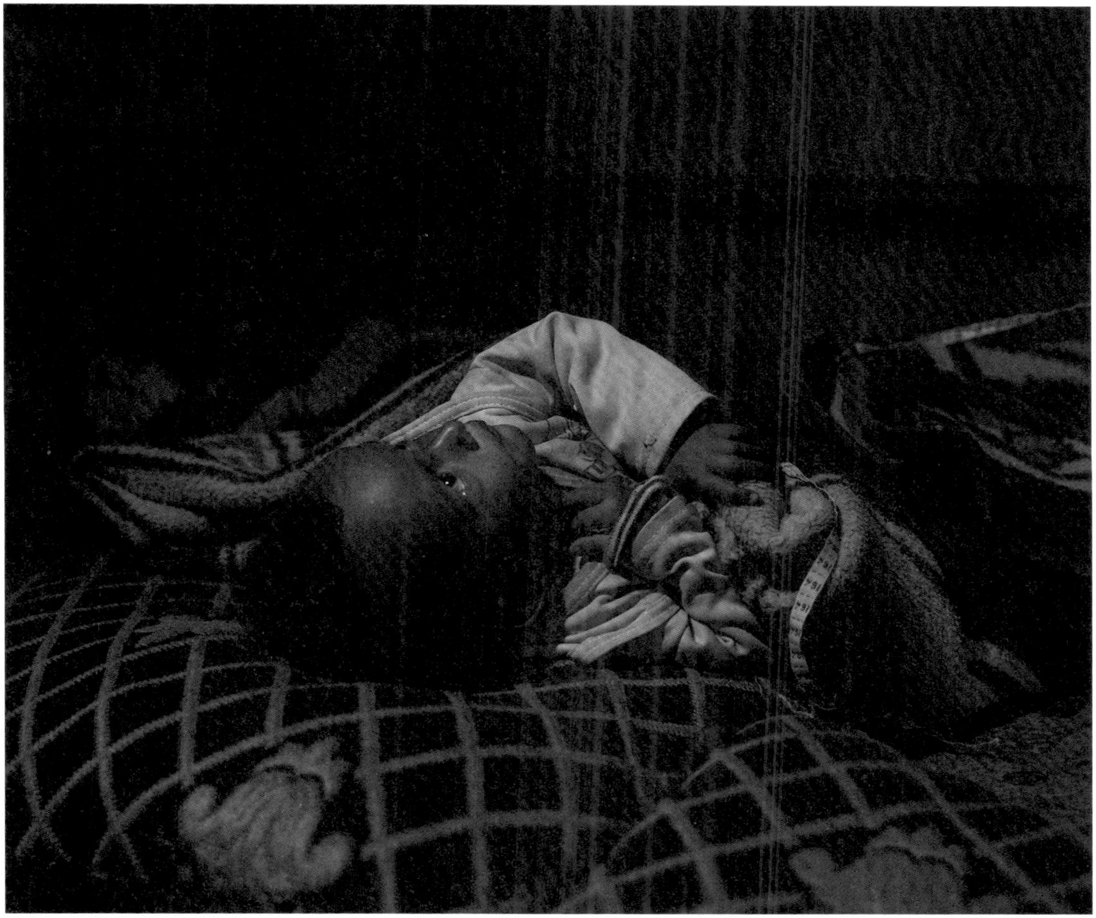

# Fara

2 years old

**AZRAQ, JORDAN.** Fara loves soccer. Her dad tries to make balls for her by crumpling up anything he can find, but they don't last long. Every night, he says goodnight to Fara and her big sister Tisam, 9, in the hope that tomorrow will bring them a proper ball to play with. All other dreams seem to be beyond his reach, but he is not giving up on this one.

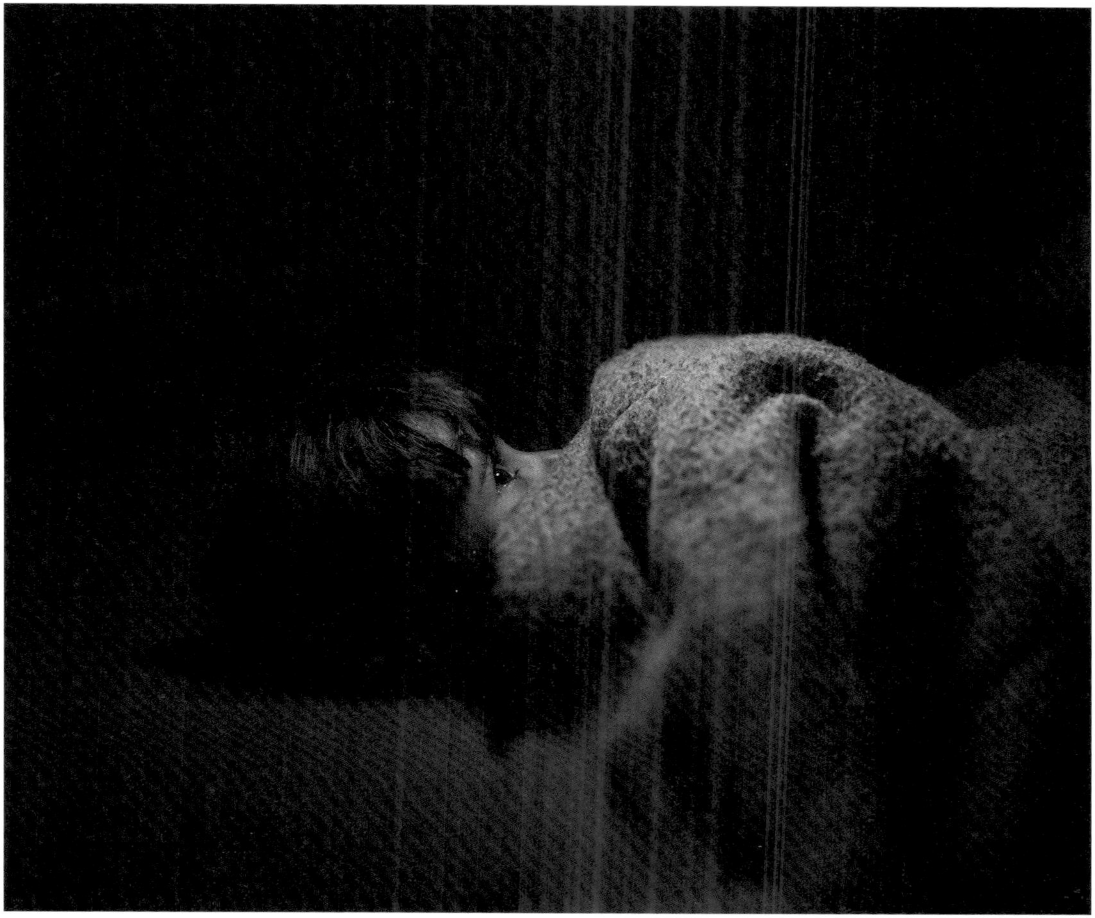

## Ahlam

8 years old

**LEIPZIG, GERMANY.** Back home in Aleppo, the Barbie dolls and the bed were left behind in the big red house. It’s them she misses most, Ahlam says. The family fled from Syria via Turkey. The smugglers took four thousand dollars to send the family with a small rubber boat across the Aegean Sea. For eight hours, the overcrowded boat drifted towards land. At Samos, sharp rocks at what the Greeks call “Death Coast” caused the boat to sink. After many hours, they were saved by two Swedish rescue boats on location in Greece. After a long journey through Europe, the whole family sits in a small room in a shabby building outside Leipzig. Ahlam has passed her first three days of school. When she grows up, she wants to be a cop. “I’ll catch all the bad guys,” she says.

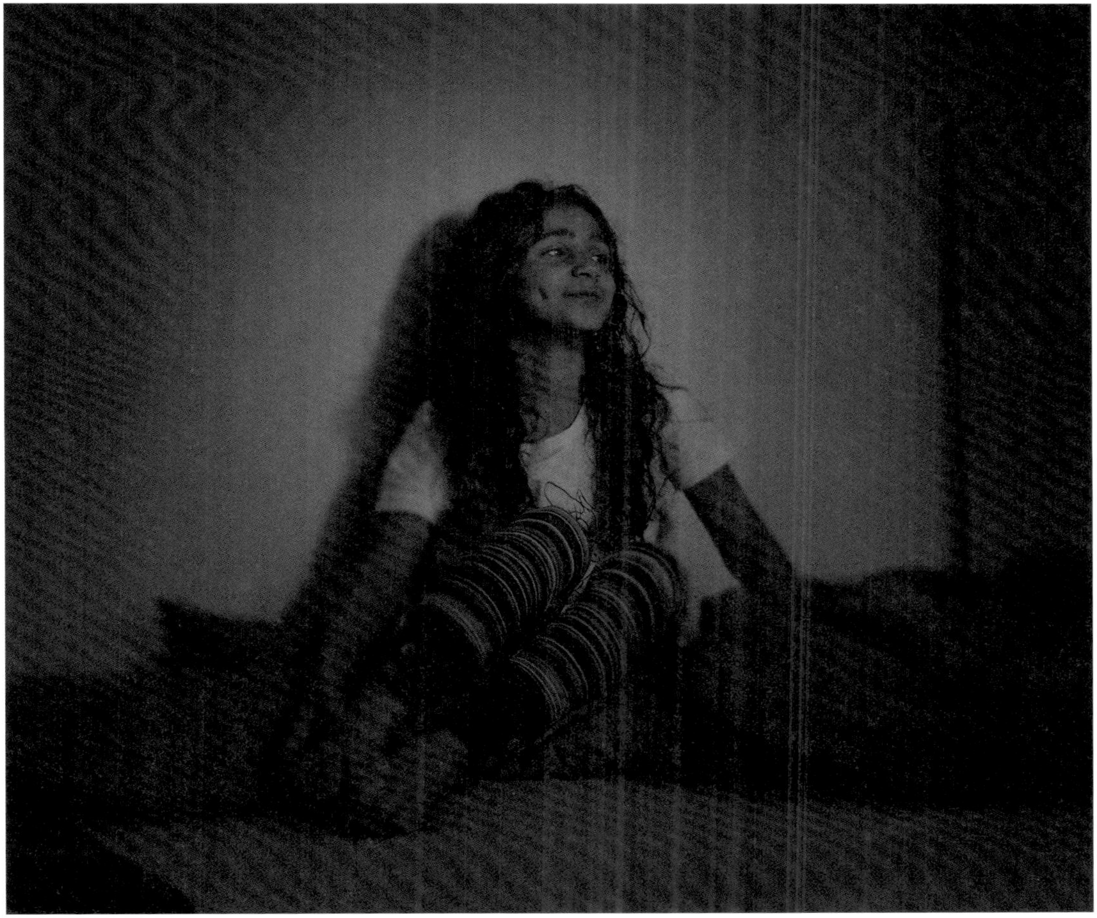

# Ali

**10 years old**

**DAR-EL-IAS, LEBANON**. Ali has a liver disease that prevents his blood from filtering as it should. As soon as he goes out in the sun, he gets severe sores, similar to burns. His mother, Turkiya, 30, has tried to get help, but it's hard. "We've been to three hospitals. At two places, they were horrified when they saw him and turned us away at the door. At the third place, we were able to see a doctor, but he couldn't do anything. He said it was too complicated," she says. Ali knows that he shouldn't go outside since his skin gets a rash. But he can't help it when he hears the others playing. "It's just so boring to only sit in the tent," he says.

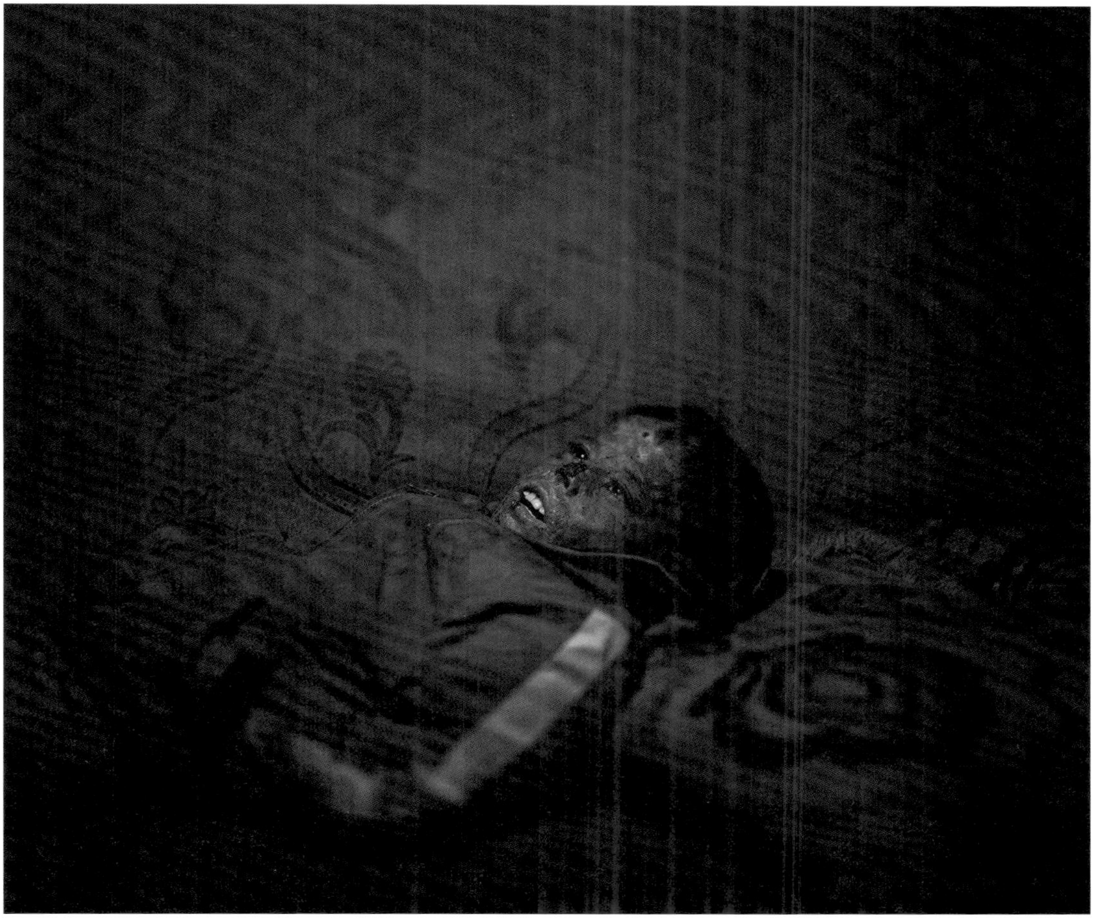

# Fatima

9 years old

**NORBERG, SWEDEN.** Every night, Fatima dreams that she's falling from a ship. Together with her mother, Malaki, and her two siblings, Fatima fled from the city of Idlib when the Syrian national army senselessly slaughtered civilians there. After two years in a refugee camp in Lebanon, the situation became unbearable and they made it to Libya, where they boarded an overcrowded boat. On the deck of the boat, a very pregnant woman gave birth to her baby after twelve hours in the scorching sun. The baby was a stillbirth and was thrown overboard. Fatima saw everything. When the refugees' boat started to take on water, they were picked up by the Italian coastguard.

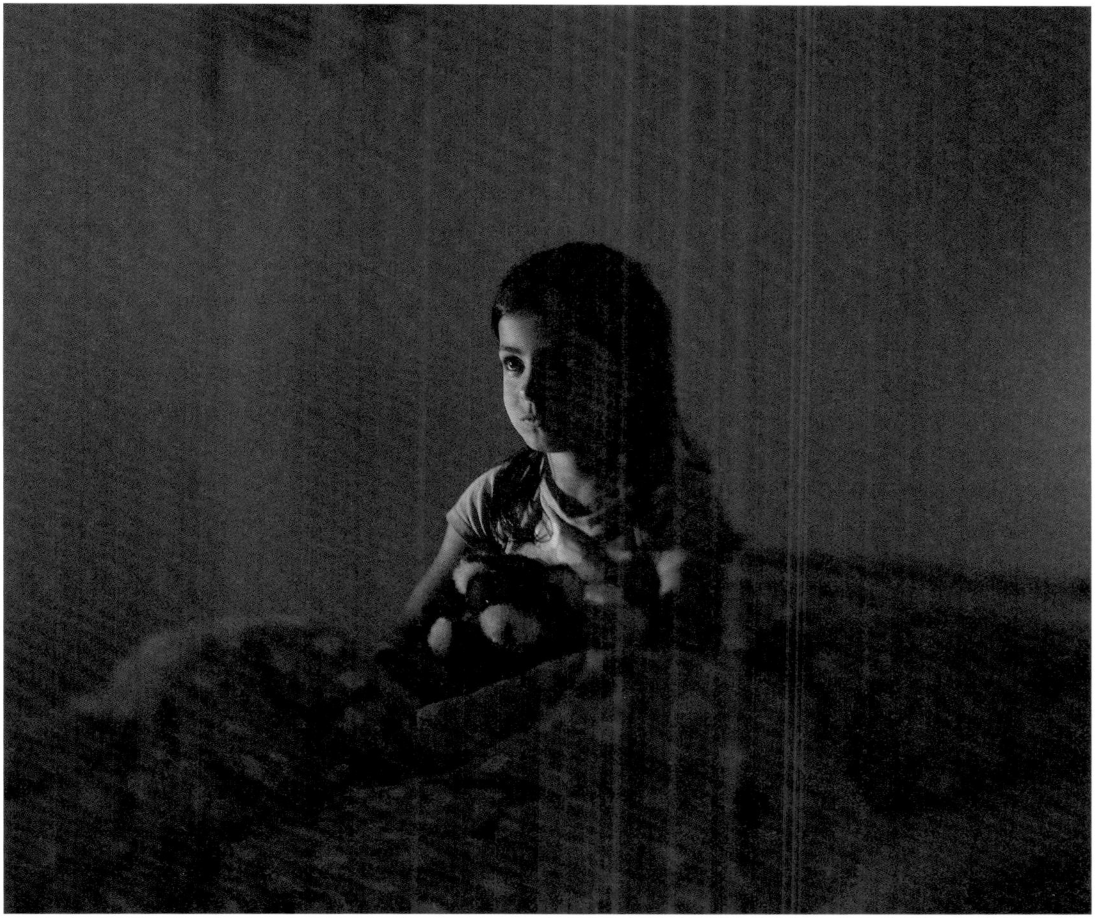

Are Monsters Real?

My six-year-old son once asked me if monsters were real. Of course not, I said. I thought about all the fathers and mothers who put their children to bed while bombs are falling outside. What would their answer be?

The project *Where the Children Sleep* began in January 2015. At that time, it was difficult to get people to care about Syria. It was a complicated war that had been going on for almost four years. But even complicated wars have innocent victims. We had to find new ways to tell their stories.

No matter how difficult this conflict may be to comprehend, it is not hard to understand that children need a safe place to sleep. I traveled to seven countries. I met children in large refugee camps, as well as in small unofficial camps. I met children who sleep in garbage dumps and on the street. I met children without parents and children who had to pick apples from the trees just to get something to eat. I met children who were forced to sleep outside a four-meter-high iron gate because the country they wanted to pass through did not want them there. What I heard most was that they were tired, that they just wanted to feel safe and to go to school again. Many mentioned that they remember the sounds of the bombings. Some of them also talked about their toys and stuffed animals that they had to leave behind.

From my experience, it takes a lot for a child to stop being a child, to stop playing and laughing; but in some cases, it felt like these children had to grow up too fast and become adults.

I could never have imagined the response that this project has received. I have mixed emotions. As a photojournalist, I want to do something that matters. I want people to see and to care. I do not always succeed—but this time, you saw and you cared.

As I am writing this, the war continues and children are forced to flee their homes every day. This book is for them.

MAGNUS WENNMAN

# Where the Children Sleep

Ever since we founded Fotografiska, we have been looking for ways to use the power of photography to unite, communicate, and initiate change in society. Today, the refugee crisis is affecting us all, and the situation has become ever-present in our day-to-day lives. We are bombarded with images of suffering and despair, setting off a global desire to help and contribute, sadly often followed by a crippling sense of helplessness and passivity.

We wanted to make a difference and we knew exactly where to turn. Magnus Wennman is one of the best photojournalists in the world. With his unique presence and rare talent, he is able to capture moments in time and create stories that resonate with people. Thus, in the fall of 2015, we joined forces with Wennman, the Swedish newspaper *Aftonbladet*, and the UNHCR to create the exhibition *Where the Children Sleep*. The idea was to create a sacred space for people to come together and hold meaningful conversations, raising the questions of what we can do to help and what kind of future we want for our children.

Through this exhibition, which was part of a wider "Fotografiska for Life" initiative, we were able to create a global discussion about children trying to escape the horrors of the war in Syria.

Following its great success, the exhibition is now traveling around the globe, being displayed in prime locations, such as New York City Public Library, the American Senate, and the United Nations, to name but a few—spreading further awareness of the refugee situation and making a positive impact in the lives of suffering children.

Serving as a social storyteller, we will continue to use the art of photography as a vehicle for conveying stories for a better future.

**JAN AND PER BROMAN,** Founders of Fotografiska

## MAGNUS WENNMAN

Born in Sweden in 1979, Magnus Wennman has been working as a photojournalist since the age of seventeen, when he started his career with a local Swedish newspaper, *Dala-Demokraten*. Since 2001, he has worked as a staff photographer at Scandinavia's largest daily newspaper, *Aftonbladet*. Wennman concentrates primarily on news and feature stories, and has worked in more than seventy countries around the world. He has won numerous prestigious photo awards, both in Sweden and abroad, including four *World Press Photo* awards, sixteen *Picture of the Year International* awards, eleven *NPPA's Best of Journalism* awards, and forty-seven *Swedish Picture of the Year* awards. He has been honored four times as *Photojournalist of the Year* in Sweden.

## Thank you

Elin & Wile, I love you.

Carina Bergfeldt, we started this together and it would never have been the same without you. So grateful I had the privilege to work with you.

Erik Wiman, my best friend and colleague.

Maria Trägårdh, Per Broman, Jan Broman, Johan Wikner, Margita Ingwall, Hans-Olav Forsang, Ann Kindahl, Fatima with family, Nour S Saeed, UNHCR, Mom, Dad.

© 2016 Kehrer Verlag Heidelberg Berlin,
Magnus Wennman, and the authors

Texts
Carina Bergfeldt, Jan and Per Broman,
Magnus Wennman, Erik Wiman

Copy Editing
Gérard A. Goodrow

Design and Image Processing
Kehrer Design Heidelberg

Production
Kehrer Design Heidelberg

The Deutsche Nationalbibliothek lists this publication in the Deutsche Nationalbibliografie; detailed bibliographic data is available on the Internet at http://dnb.de.

Printed and bound in Germany

ISBN 978-3-86828-724-0

Kehrer Heidelberg Berlin
www.kehrerverlag.com

IN COOPERATION WITH

Sverige för UNHCR FN:s flyktingorgan

Fotografiska

AFTONBLADET

If you wish to support the work of the UNHCR, you can make a donation at
http://donate.unhcr.org